The BANT
Frameworks

by

Josef Reisz

This Sales Pocket Guide is a concise, easy-to-read book with actionable tips and insights that will help you get more business.

The BANT method and SPIN technique are two popular sales methodologies that help you structure your questions during a sale to help you qualify your prospects by:

- Situation

- Problem

- Impact

- Need-Payoff

- Budget

- Authority

- Need

- Timescale

Each comes with its own set of questions, but be aware that the quality of the question is more important than the number you ask

This Sales Pocket Guide is your valuable companion in every sales call & conversation you will have.

Go back to this back every time before you make that call, and see you hit (and exceed!) your targets. Every single month!

About Josef Reisz

Josef Reisz is a CEO with over 25 years of experience in the development of new markets, strategic planning and implementation.

Josef has been on both sides of the table; as an Entrepreneur, he started out by founding six successful companies, such as VU Capital, JRC Strategic Business Advisory and, most recently, HoneyComb Agency.

He also has extensive experience working for Fortune 500 corporations as well as smaller privately-owned businesses - holding various roles such as Head of Sales, Marketing and eCommerce.

Josef Reisz is a serial entrepreneur with an impressive track record. He has had experience in various roles on the C- and Board level held positions as Head of Sales, Head of Marketing, Head of Ecommerce, CEO, Non-Exec and Advisory Board member.

Josef has written five books on topics ranging from personal growth to business success. His writings have helped countless people build better lives while growing their respective brands or companies.

About HoneyComb

HoneyComb is A Team Of Creative Strategists Who Love Crafting Beautiful, Smart And Inspired Strategies That Help Businesses Meet Their Most Ambitious Objectives.

HoneyComb provides In-Depth training with a proven track-record for sales team that enables them to hit their targets, stay motivated and incentivised, close more deals and generate more, predictable revenue for your organisation.

Fast-track Transformation of Organisations And Teams Into Well-Oiled, Homogenous And Inspired Powerhouses By Strategic Design.

www.HoneyCombAgency.co.uk

HONEYCOMB

Introduction

The BANT method and SPIN technique are two popular sales methodologies that help you structure your questions during a sale. Each comes with its own set of questions, but be aware that the quality of the question is more important than the number you ask.

Your prospect can tell if you don't listen to their answers or understand their questions, and this can damage the sale.

It's important to not lose sight of your overall goals during a Q&A session. Your objective is always to ask questions that lead you closer to closing the deal, so here are some tips on how to do just that.

HoneyComb has developed its very own sales methodology which is partly based on SPIN, BANT and other frameworks which have proven track records over the past 30 years.

Active Listening

Before we dive deep into SPIN and BANT sales frameworks, I would like to emphasise the importance of Active Listening.

In every sales conversation you will have, active listening is the bedrock of your success. Regularly think about what the customer is saying while they are talking and really open yourself up to hearing their concerns.

Think about how your prospect is feeling and whether they're in need of empathy before you show them understanding. Understanding their feelings can lead you to a sale because it shows them that you care rather than that you just want to sell something.

More importantly:

Make notes consistently throughout your sales call (or conversation, thereof). Notice what terminology your prospect uses, their tonality, their choice of words and phrases, their speed of speech.

Why is that important? Because you want to build rapport in the conversation and get into a natural flow. By utilising certain NLP - Neuro-Linguistic Programming - techniques, you will be able to build that rapport and connect with your prospect on a deeper level without being intrusive. NLP is built up from a few fundamental principles:

People already have all the resources they need. The mind and body are interconnected in some mysterious ways. You can change your life by changing your state of mind.

Using those ideas as a basis, you can then display - and more importantly: mirror - certain behaviours that will increase the likelihood of getting into rapport with someone.

The SPIN sales methodology is a customer-focused approach that helps organisations identify the problem and all possible, relevant solutions. One of the keys to success when using this method is understanding your prospect's "hot buttons" and how they are affected by 'pain'.

Building Rapport

Building rapport with your prospect is a prerequisite of having a meaningful, customer-centric conversation. Rapport is the psychological and mental connection between two people who are in alignment with each other.

You can build rapport by showing credibility and capability, or in other words: becoming your prospect's trusted advisor during your conversation.

On top of that, one tip that helped me a lot personally over the past 25 years in sales: Act as if your prospect were already a business acquaintance. By mentally preparing yourself in such a way, you will never think that you could potentially waste their time because you're cold calling them. Here are a few more, simple rapport building techniques:

Start with a sincere compliment and then follow it up with an open-ended question. The best compliments are typically about their business because people love talking about themselves, and it's not directly related to buying your product.

Don't ask too many questions at once. You want to have the other person participate in the conversation as much as possible. Ask them one or two questions and let them answer fully before diving into more questions so that they can share their perspective on what you're asking about. This will also help you to avoid having long pauses in the conversation when you start giving them time for answers, which is usually perceived as awkwardness by most people.

Ethos - Pathos - Logos

It is important to know your influencer style as a sales person because it will have an influence on how you lead your conversations. It will also be important to know what your audience's influencer style is.

There are three key "influencer" styles to consider during sales conversations: Pathos, Ethos and Logos. This refers to the way in which we allow ourselves to be influenced by other people. The chart below shows how these styles work with each other - for example if you use a pathos approach (emotion) it can increase your ethos (likeability), but decrease logos (logic)

As a Sales Person, when you think about your own style, try and become self-aware of where you sit on this axis. If you don't know what that means then that's OK! Think about it this way though...

Have you ever had a sales conversation with someone where you were talking about how good your product or service was and they weren't listening? You started to feel disrespected and annoyed...did it make you less likely to buy from them?

As a customer, have you ever had a sales person who is clearly disinterested in what they are selling provide information about their product or service? It makes you wonder if the staff even use the product/service themselves...or worse still, if they're just trying to sell something that's not right for you. This can make customers less interested as well!

Pathos - Be real

Be passionate but also be honest about your company and what it can offer. Use an empathetic approach so that the customer feels included and wants to do business with you

Ethos - Be likeable

Be friendly, be approachable but also make people feel confident in your company so that they want to do business with you. This can be done by reinforcing positive traits about your product or service and repeating the message across various mediums

Logos - Be knowledgeable

When we use logos, sales people are trying to present their product/service as the best solution compared to other products/services available on the market. Businesses who have effective logos selling strategies tend to avoid making a big emotional connection as this can distract from the fact that they are trying to sell a logical choice!

So how does all of this help us in real life? Well, for starters, you need to be aware of these influencer styles when trying to influence a customer. You also need to be self-aware and understand where your own style sits within this spectrum. If it's not beneficial then change your approach as soon as possible!

Do you want to know how you are being influenced during a sales conversation? Take the questionnaire below which was developed by Cialdini:

"Which one of the following statements do you most agree with?"

1. "I think people like me"

2. "I am really quite lovable."

3. I will probably like them very much if I get to know them better"

4. "People won't like me very much."

5. "I am pretty certain that I won't like them very much."

If you answered 1 or 2 then your pathos is influencing you. You need to think of an approach that works with all three styles (pathos, ethos and logos) if you want to make the sale.

If you answered 3 or 4 then your logos is influencing you but it's created by your pathos! In this scenario, try and create a stronger connection with your customer using an empathetic approach so they feel like they really understand what makes them tick. Use emotion when discussing how their life will be better after purchasing.

If you answered 5 then your ethos is influencing you but it's been created by your logos!

SPIN

The SPIN Sales Methodology is a sales methodology that was developed by Neil Rackham to help his company increase their prospecting and closing rate. SPIN stands for Situation, Problem, Implication and Need-payoff.

SPIN is focused on making sure the customer understands the problem they have in relation to your product or service before you present them with solutions.

The SPIN sales methodology is a customer-focused approach that helps organisations identify the problem and all possible, relevant solutions.

SPIN has been proven to be an effective way of increasing prospecting rates because it starts with understanding what the customer needs rather than what your business can offer them.

SPIN is focused on the customer's needs rather than what your organisation can offer them.

According to Rackham, this is because successful salespeople spend more time talking about the customer's problems rather than their own products and services. This is contrary to the common sales methodology of focus on products and services, features and benefits.

Features are irrelevant until you have uncovered your prospect's Situation, Need and Implications on their business when sticking with the status quo.

Sales people who apply the SPIN methodology have proven to be more effective in uncovering needs.

According to research:

When you're talking about your product or service, you're making assumptions. You may assume that the prospect wants a faster machine because their current one is too slow and have presented them with features as benefits.

However they might be looking for better quality due to excess breakdowns so they don't benefit from faster speeds.

During a conversation, if you and the prospect go on about their business (what they do), then your product or service (what you do) there is a high chance that this will not be beneficial for either of you. It is your job as a sales person - or shall I say: Business Consultant - to use your expertise to help uncover the real problem so you can deliver a solution that will be beneficial to both of you.

Remember, if it doesn't benefit them, they don't care!

The SPIN Sales Methodology is based around four steps:

Situation

Establish a problem, identify it and then assess its significance to the prospect.

You as the sales person want to know what problems your prospect have that need solving; not just which product or service you can sell.

Situation questions aim at finding out exactly what the prospect's business situation is, their set up in terms of technology, organisational structure and future roadmaps.

Situation questions are the foundation of your call structure with prospects. It enables you to understand where your prospects are in their journey and where they want to go.

SPIN is all about helping prospects move forward, not remaining stagnant. SPIN's Situation questions are designed to help your prospect get clarity on their situation and then identify the major issues they're facing in that arena.

This allows you to determine what problems need solving for them and why your product can solve it better than any other solution or service provider.

Evaluating your prospect's Situation is important because you want to know what their business feels like, not just what the numbers and facts are.

Only by understanding your prospect's environment can you truly determine what problems exist for them and why they need a solution.

This requires you to ask questions that will uncover the reasons why certain issues exist in their current situation.

By asking detailed questions after you have defined the problem, you will learn more about how it affects your prospect's business and strategy.

The Situation stage is essential for you to gather insights into your prospect's business environment and ideally their strategy and culture.

By matching your prospect's Situation with your own Value Proposition, spontaneously during your conversation, you are in a position to highlight how your product fits into their current strategy and how they can benefit from your proposition at the right time in your sales conversation.

This is significant because it demonstrates your credibility and builds trust with your prospect while letting them know that you have done your homework and fully understand their industry.

In order to gather the necessary information about a prospect's business situation, you need to ask specific questions pertaining to their current strategy, priorities, vision, goals and issues.

You can also ask questions to understand their current and future needs, constraints, expectations as well as potential influences.

With this stage you need to make sure that all of your assumptions are confirmed during the conversation.

Your prospect may have different values, visions, strategies, and issues and if you are unable to recognise this during the call or meeting then it will be clear that your value proposition doesn't meet their expectations or needs.

A lack of situational information during your conversation can result in lack of rapport and a poor understanding of their business prior to purchase.

With this you won't know how to approach the rest of the sales process, causing confusion and potentially a loss of potential revenue for you.

Gather insights into your prospect's business environment in order to understand their strategy and needs.

Make sure you ask the right specific questions based on your initial assumptions in your sales script.

Examples

- *How are you currently dealing with ...?*

- *What does your strategy for the next 12 months look like?*

- *How are you using XYZ in your organisation?*

- *What is your general approach for ...?*

- *How do you plan on assessing the ROI of XYZ?*

- *When are you planning to make a decision about ...?*

- *What factors will influence this decision?*

- *In what areas do you feel like the success of XYZ will be measured in terms of return on investment (ROI)?*

Problem

Identify the problem or opportunity that needs solving

The Problem stage is the second phase of Neil Rackham's SPIN model. This is where you identify and uncover the problem that your prospect has in relation to your product or service.

You also need to make sure they understand how significant this problem is to them - it should be making their business realise that something needs changing because they have been dealing with this issue for too long!

When uncovering the problem - and by utilising carefully drafted and formulated sets of questions - you need to make clear what solution it requires, what type of solution (uniqueness) and how it will compete against existing market solutions.

With specific problem questions, you can find out what our prospects have been struggling with currently and in the past.

This allows you to determine what problems need solving for them and why your product can solve it better than any other solution or service provider. It is important to ensure that you have a good grasp of how your product or service can help them and why they should consider changing from their existing supplier.

In addition, it is crucial that you identify what pain points they are currently experiencing to ensure no other companies can solve it better (e.g., lower costs) and that the problem isn't just a priority, but needs addressing immediately.

Once you have uncovered and defined the problem(s) that you prospect is/has experiencing, it's now time to provide an explanation of how your company's solution can help them.

This could include quantifiable metrics (e.g., savings), project timelines and details of any additional services that could be provided.

Here it is important to understand the uniqueness behind your product and why it's different from anything else in the market - so don't forget to highlight its advantages!

It is also a good idea at this point to show how your product can bypass existing competitive solutions by answering any objections they may have about your product or service.

Examples

- *How has [INSERT TRIGGER EVENT] affected your business?*

- *How difficult is it for you to do xxx?*

- *How time consuming is it for you...?*

- *How long does it take you to do ...?*

- *What effects on your business do you expect from [TRIGGER EVENT]?*

- *What do you think is causing this issue?*

- *How would a change make a difference here?*

- *Why has this been an ongoing challenge for you?*

Implication

Explore and/or quantify how big an issue this is for your prospects, what they think of it, why it's important, and what the implications would be if they remained with their status quo.

Identify the implications of not resolving the problem, and then show them how they will benefit from solving it.

Prospects don't care about problems they have unless the implications of not dealing with them are high enough that it could disrupt their business operations. So at this stage you need to show them how important solving the problem is.

As your conversation progresses through asking SPIN questions, you will learn more about your prospect's business in relation to your product or service.

Questions in the Implication stage give you more focus and help you - and your prospect - to understand how important the problem is as well as what may happen if your prospect carries on with the status quo.

The Implication stage is about demonstrating to prospects that there are more negatives in failing to act on a problem than positives.

They need to understand that if nothing is done, their business will remain stuck in its current situation without progress; this could mean declines in performance, market share, productivity etc.

You need to make sure your prospect sees the disadvantages of sticking with their current status quo rather than obtaining a permanent fix through your product or service. You also want them to see how

This is one of the trickiest parts of SPIN. The aim here is to assess your prospects perception of the problem you have found in Step 2, how significant this problem really is and what its implications are for their business if they don't address it now or in the foreseeable future.

It's important to remember that there are many problems with dire consequences - some small ones can be just as detrimental to your prospect's business so make sure you test both waters here!

This step also involves understanding the factors behind the implication (i.e. why should they care?) - what's driving this problem? Why will situation X change if situation Y does not alter?

In order for them to understand exactly why they need to start the change - and, ideally, use your solution to do so - you need to clearly demonstrate the importance of their problem and its implications on their business, their bottom-line, their market share, etc.

Examples

- *How much is it costing you to do XYZ the way you're doing it right now?*

- *How difficult is it for you currently to predict XYZ?*

- *What effects on your business do you expect from XYZ?*

- *What will happen to your market share and revenue?*

- *How else would you expect this issue to erode profitability of your business throughout 2017?*

- *What impact will this have on your ability to enter new markets and sell products/services as a result of...?*

- *What do you think will happen if...?*

- *What changes do you expect your customers to make as a result?*

- *What is the likelihood that they will...?*

- *What effects on your business would you expect from ...?*

- *How difficult or inconvenient / time consuming is it for you to do*

- *How is this impacting other areas of your business?*

Need-Payoff

Determine your prospects need by identifying where they are now (Situation), where they want to be (Objectives) and how they can get there with your solution (Bridging the Gap)

The Need-Payoff is about showing a clear path that leads from their current situation (Step 1) through objectives (Step 2) and over a bridge consisting of your product or service (Step 3)

It's important that this bridge is a strong one.

Find out what they have tried in the past, why it didn't work, and what results they were expecting from this course of action.

Let your prospect describe to you how they are performing currently. Show them where they are at right now and what steps they need to take to hit their objectives.

Bridging the Gap: How can you help your prospects get from where they are now to where you think they should be?

A Need-Payoff question, as opposed to a simple Need question, provides the sales person with the opportunity to refer to the prospect's objectives, desired outcomes and the method of getting there.

The Need-Payoff is a very powerful question to ask during your SPIN questioning when the prospect has already indicated some level of interest in solving their problem.

It will help you better understand exactly what your prospect's needs are, what the implications of not solving them would be and how they believe they can go about doing this (as expressed in their objectives and desired outcomes).

After asking a Need-Payoff question, you will want to show that your solution can help them reach their end goal (their objectives or desired outcomes) by providing the appropriate information on how to get there and how your solution will be of benefit in this scenario.

Examples

"If we could demonstrate that we could help you to increase productivity by 10%, and you would generate an extra $1 million per month for your company. How would that affect your bottom-line?"

Or:

"If we could demonstrate to you that we could help you to reduce staff turnover by 10%, that means there will be less time spent hiring and training new employees, what would that mean for your cash flow and bottom-line results?"

The important word in this part is 'Payoff'.

A need without a payoff, i.e. something to justify the efforts involved in meeting that need, is not satisfactory.

The payoff should reflect on their bottom-line, cash flow or other financial KPIs and business drivers. Remember: In the end, business decision are financial decisions. In 25 years, I have yet to see a company that makes a purchase without knowing the ROI of their decision.

The benefits need to be clear, and focused on specific metrics such as KPIs (Key Performance Indicators), financial or otherwise.

Remember that there is a positive correlation between specificity and impact - the more specific you can be about what will happen if they go for your solution, the greater its potential impact upon them.

BANT

The BANT sales methodology provides a structure of relevant sales qualifying questions that help sales people qualify their prospects for Budget, Authority, Need and Timescale.

It helps you get a good overview of your prospect's situation so that you make sure the solution you are selling is actually what they need. Your questions should be open-ended and focus on understanding their business as a whole rather than a particular aspect or department.

Questioning your prospects with BANT questions will help surface any potential issues that they may have. This could be anything from cash-flows problems, lack of people or authority, gaining budgets etc

These questions not only help you to qualify prospects but also give a good understanding of your prospect's needs and how he will perceive your product/service.

This is a good technique to use for sales people just starting out as it provides them with all the relevant questions they might need to ask their prospects. A senior person in the business who knows every area will have no problem of course, but a newer rep cannot be expected to know how each prospect ticks so this can help him structure his questioning and therefore get better answers.

In a nutshell, BANT stands for Budget, Authority, Need and Timeframe:

B - Budget means do they have money to spend on our solution?

A - Authority refers to how much power does the person you are selling to actually have? Can he make decisions on spending money without sending it down another level first, who needs to approve that etc.?

N - Need is what problems are they trying to solve and what's missing in their situation? Do they need better cash flow or maybe less downtime for example. How urgent is this?

T - Timeframe is when do they need your solution by.

Why is it important for you as a sales person to know these things about your prospect and their business?

Well, it helps you to qualify whether your prospect is a good fit for your offering. It also lets you know how they are likely to perceive it so that you can tailor your solution towards them if necessary.

You then have much more of an idea as to what's important to them and why.

If the answers don't match up with what you're selling, or even worse, they aren't interested in buying anything at all, then there's no point wasting any more of their time. Or yours.

Budget

Nobody likes to talk about money.

But you're a sales person and it is your job to understand if your prospect has a budget or would be able to get it. It's really important that you don't promise something you can't deliver.

If your prospect hasn't got a budget available, think of some ways to indicate the value they could get from your product or service so that they would be interested in getting consultations and evaluations

Example: "Is this project/report something that is going to require additional funding or budget sources?" It's really important to know how much is available for your project or to see if the prospect you're talking with has a budget at all.

So it's important that you ask.

Do not avoid to ask your prospect this question as it will be a deciding factor for your sales. If your prospect hasn't got a budget available, think of some ways to indicate the value they could get from your product or service so that they would be interested in getting consultations and evaluations.

You don't want to waste time on selling a product that has no budget. Also if the customer knows you don't have an idea about their budget, you will lose their trust and they may simply decline the offer.

The power has shifted from the seller-side to the buyer-side these days. Asking specific questions, including about the budget, shows that you take your own business serious. Hence, you show authority and credibility.

However, don't just ask them what the amount of their budget is. Of course they want to spend as little money as possible, but that doesn't mean your product or service fulfil all their needs. That's why it's super important to also discuss

A good question to ask could be:

"Hypothetically, if you were to believe that our solution would add value to your business, how could budget be allocated to start our partnership?"

Answers to this question could be: *"We have a specific budget for that kind of projects"*, or *"We want to start with a smaller amount and maybe increase our investment"*.

Whatever the answer, it shows that your prospect has a budget and is able to allocate resources. Ideally.

It shows that they trust you. That's why asking about the budget will be a deciding factor for your sales as it proves to them that you take your own business serious and have authority and credibility.

Naturally, there will be times when a prospect tells you that they would not share this information before having seen more evidence or a proposal. Again, that is fine. You can always revert back to the 'hypothetical' scenario.

Another way around a situation like this would be to ask:

"How did you handle a project like this in the past? Just to give me an idea..."

Authority

Questions about authority help you understand what levels in an organisation are involved in decision making.

Sending sales people into organisations without this knowledge is like sending soldiers onto a battlefield without a strategy or direction.

You need to know which departments you will be speaking with and at what level.

Who makes decisions in the organisation?

Will your prospect have authority over purchase whatever it is you're selling?

Do they need approval from anyone else or are they able to make their own decisions?

You don't want your sale blocked because you do not know or understand your prospect's decision making process.

Need

It's important that you uncover an undeniable need with your prospect and their business.

The purpose of getting on a call with someone is to establish

- *Does your solution fit their needs? If not, what other potential solutions might they need or want that you may offer*

- *Or, what other solutions are they evaluating at the moment?*

In gathering, once you get an idea of what it is exactly that they're looking for and how it fits into their current strategy, environment, business culture etc., be sure to validate why this is important to them

This is an easy way for you to understand what problems your prospect faces, how this problem may be holding back other aspects of their business and whether or not they see this problem as a priority worth investing in.

But don't overcomplicate things. This is typically very simple and straightforward.

Understanding their needs will be at the heart of your sales process moving forward, so make sure to really dig deep here.

Execute fast, continue to gather data, prioritise actions based on what they tell you about their business environment (cycle time between ideas and execution, risk profile of their environment, etc).

Make sure you have a good understanding of the problem and potential business value before you spend time on any proposition.

Remember: We don't prioritise anything without first clarifying the problem and explicit need.

Make sure you get the full picture and leave no stone unturned before moving onto the next step.

But what if there is no explicit need at the moment? In that case, the deal is (still) not lost. Sometimes, it is all about timing, and the timing might just not be the right one at this particular moment. Is the deal lost, therefore?

Not at all. Even without a Need identified, your last resort is to provide your prospect with further information on your Value Proposition and a follow up after an agreed timeframe.

All of the information that you've gathered up until now will determine how much time you need to dedicate to developing a solution proposal, which brings us to our next point:

Understanding your prospect's company culture.

Company Culture

The company culture can give you valuable insights into your prospect's buying process and decision making.

It also helps you understand if there is alignment between what their company wants and what they are actually buying.

These insights can give you a great upper hand when negotiating, because it allows you to close more deals by helping your prospect with their internal problems.

In many companies the buying process goes through multiple layers of management.

For example:

Your prospect might be a director in a company, but the actual purchase decision will be handed down to his manager.

During your initial conversations you might not be aware of this dynamic and as a result start talking about features and benefits, which won't lead to any progress.

If you are lucky enough to have found out who is actually making the buying decision let's go through a few questions you should ask to find out more about them:

- *What is their main responsibility?*

- *What are the biggest challenges in their job/ department right now?*

- *Is it a growth company or rather reluctant to change?How and where is your prospect positioned in the company?*

- *Do they report to a board or rather work independently?*

- *What are their future career plans?*

- *Who else would be involved in the purchasing decision? (Vendors, colleagues, etc.)*

- *What was the last book that made an impact on them personally (emotional connection)*

- *What are the biggest challenges they have had to deal with in their role?*

Some of these questions will help you understand your prospect's professional needs, some might reveal additional people that need to be involved, while others will show you if there is alignment between what your company can offer and what would actually make a positive improvement for them.

The answers will also give you insights into the type of person you're dealing with and how they like to be approached.

Remember: most employees working in a company have multiple roles and responsibilities, so don't expect them to know everything about their department or the problems they're trying to solve. It might be just as effective talking to one of the

Another important consideration to gain insights into your prospect's company: What types of decisions have been made in the past?

Do they tend to go big and fully buy into new ideas/solutions? Or are they more skeptical about change and trying new things out? Understanding their organisation's decision-making style will help you tailor your pitch accordingly.

Do they tend to buy from vendors that have a broad portfolio of service or do they value tailored services such as those offered by your company?

Do they have pre-existing relationships with other companies that might present a conflict of interest for your company?

Are they looking for solutions from you that compliment those of their partners or vendors?

Be sure to address the difficulties, questions and objections as many times as necessary until you get full commitment. Be patient but persistent. If there is any resistance at all try to find out why before going ahead with the solution proposal etc.

But don't take it personally if your prospect occasionally balks at an idea or hesitates on something you've proposed. It's easy to reject an idea when considering it in isolation and not within the context of all the other factors involved in solving their problem/need; finding out what those are will help you sell more effectively.

Timescale

Lastly, you need to gather information on whether your prospect has an active project where you could fit in, or a project in the future.

And if so, what is your prospect's anticipated timeline: When is the projected start of the project, when is it due?

How long does it usually take for your prospect's organisation to buy services or products like yours? 3 months, 6 months, 12 months?And does your prospect's company operate on a fiscal year?

Once these questions are answered, you're now ready to take the prospect to the next level with you.

And does your prospect's company operate on a fiscal year budget?

When you have all this information, it will help you determine what your follow up action should be. It may be a good idea to set a date for the next meeting/call with your prospect and then send an email summarising everything discussed during your conversation or make a proposal in case some of the details are missing.

But perhaps most importantly, you need to have a clear idea of whether your prospect is still in the market for what you're offering.

Many salespeople assume that if the customers don't buy now, there is no point staying in touch. But this is usually because those people didn't fully investigate their prospects' needs during their conversations and as such did not get a chance to develop an effective solution proposal.

Conclusion

The BANT and SPIN sales frameworks are two commonly used qualifying models that are considered by many salespeople to be industry standards.

Neither of these methods, however, is as effective and accurate as they could be

Instead of using a one size fits all approach, sales professionals should focus on building each individual customer relationship based on their unique needs through consultative selling.

The BANT framework provides a general roadmap toward helping you qualify your leads for your specific product/service

It can also serve as a good foundation when adding more detailed questions to the SPIN model; the more information you know about your prospect and their company, the better equipped you are in making an offer they can't refuse.

Remember: it's not just about asking the right questions at the right time but understanding what your prospect is really asking when they respond and getting them to elaborate, which is perhaps the greatest challenge of all.

And always keep in mind that there are no right or wrong answers; if you get an answer you don't expect, it's only because you need to probe further

The more information you have about your prospect, the more qualified they will be for working with you.

Printed in Great Britain
by Amazon

66016695R00031